U.S. HISTORY TIMELINES

Civil War
1856-1865

Jack Zayarny

MEDIA ENHANCED BOOKS
AV2
BY WEIGL™
ADDED VALUE • AUDIO VISUAL

www.av2books.com

AV² provides enriched content that supplements and complements this book. Weigl's AV² books strive to create inspired learning and engage young minds in a total learning experience.

Your AV² Media Enhanced books come alive with...

Audio
Listen to sections of the book read aloud.

Key Words
Study vocabulary, and complete a matching word activity.

Video
Watch informative video clips.

Quizzes
Test your knowledge.

Embedded Weblinks
Gain additional information for research.

Slide Show
View images and captions, and prepare a presentation.

Try This!
Complete activities and hands-on experiments.

... and much, much more!

Go to **www.av2books.com**, and enter this book's unique code.

BOOK CODE

N 5 9 2 5 1 3

AV² by Weigl brings you media enhanced books that support active learning.

Published by AV² by Weigl
350 5th Avenue, 59th Floor
New York, NY 10118
Websites: www.av2books.com   www.weigl.com

Library of Congress Control Number: 2014933469
ISBN 978–1–4896–0728–7 (hardcover)
ISBN 978–1–4896–0729–4 (softcover)
ISBN 978–1–4896–0730–0 (single–user eBook)
ISBN 978–1–4896–0731–7 (multi–user eBook)

Printed in the United States of America in North Mankato, Minnesota
1 2 3 4 5 6 7 8 9 0   18 17 16 15 14

052014
WEP090514

Project Coordinator: Aaron Carr
Editor: Pamela Dell
Designer: Mandy Christiansen

Every reasonable effort has been made to trace ownership and to obtain permission to reprint copyright material. The publishers would be pleased to have any errors or omissions brought to their attention so that they may be corrected in subsequent printings.

Weigl acknowledges Getty Images as its primary image supplier for this title.

CONTENTS

A Nation Divided

By the mid-1800s, the United States had engaged in two wars with Great Britain. It had become an independent nation, no longer under British control. Now, it was important to keep the country strong and united. However, the serious issue of slavery divided the American people. Some states had **abolished** slavery. Others, mostly in the South, supported the practice. This created tensions between the states in favor of slavery and those against it.

The southern states wanted to ensure that the right to own slaves would not be taken away. Others wanted slavery abolished throughout the country. To unite as a nation, the United States needed to resolve the issue of slavery. In the 1856 election, this issue took center stage.

COTTON PLANTATIONS THROUGHOUT the South depended heavily on slave labor.

1856 PRESIDENTIAL ELECTION

In the U.S. presidential election of 1856, three parties ran against each other. The Republicans were against expanding slavery. The Democrats argued that this extreme view would lead to **civil war**. The American Party, or the "Know-Nothings," ignored the issue of slavery altogether. The Democrats won with the election of James Buchanan.

DRED SCOTT DECISION, 1857

In 1857, the U.S. Supreme Court brought a decision in the Dred Scott case. By this decision, slaves, former slaves, and descendants of slaves were to have no right to citizenship.

Dred Scott was an enslaved man who moved north into free territory with his owners. In 1857, Scott sued to win his freedom. He argued that since he now lived in the free North, he was a free man. The U.S. Supreme Court voted 7 to 2 against Scott.

HARPER'S FERRY RAID, 1859

John Brown was a dedicated **abolitionist**. On October 17, 1859, Brown led a raid on Harper's Ferry, Virginia. The men raided the United States **armory** there. They planned to distribute weapons to slaves and freedom fighters. The plan failed. Brown and his men were easily captured. Brown was hanged for treason less than two months later.

FUGITIVE SLAVES

Fugitive Slave laws of 1850 and before declared that anyone who helped escaping slaves would be harshly punished. Most people in the **free states** opposed these laws, whereas most southerners did not. This added to the tensions between North and South

The Rise of Lincoln

Abraham Lincoln was a lawyer and politician from Illinois. In 1860, the newly formed Republican Party nominated Lincoln for president. Not widely known, Lincoln impressed people with his passionate views and intelligent and articulate way of expressing those views. Many Republicans also favored Lincoln for his reluctance to expand slavery.

Lincoln quickly gained supporters, who backed him at the polls against presidential candidates Stephen A. Douglas, John Bell, and John C. Breckinridge. On November 6, 1860, Lincoln was elected 16th president of the United States. He was the first-ever Republican president, winning 180 **electoral** votes. He also received 40 percent of the **popular vote**.

In the following months, several southern states **seceded** from the rest of the **Union**. These states, all of which supported slavery, were South Carolina, Mississippi, Florida, Alabama, Georgia, Louisiana, and Texas.

| 1856–1859 | 1860 | 1861 | 1861 | 1861 | 1862 |

HON. ABRAHAM LINCOLN, OF ILLINOIS.

FOR PRESIDENT.

HON. HANNIBAL HAMLIN, OF MAINE,

FOR VICE PRESIDENT.

LINCOLN AND HIS running mate, Hannibal Hamlin, promised more than just abolishing slavery. Lincoln promised a coast-to-coast railway system. He also called for a "Homestead Act," which would give free land to settlers.

Formation of the Confederacy

On February 4, 1861, the southern states decided to form their own nation. This nation was to be called the **Confederate** States of America. The members of the Confederacy, as it became known, opposed Lincoln's desire to limit the expansion of slavery. They intended to keep slavery and were against giving African Americans equal rights.

U.S. **senator** Jefferson Davis was named president of the Confederate States on February 9, 1861. He wanted a peaceful separation from the United States of America, but this was not to be. Lincoln viewed the secession as an illegal rebellion. He felt this justified his taking action against these states.

This led to further rebellion. At 4:30 AM on April 12, 1861, Confederate forces attacked Fort Sumter in Charleston, South Carolina. The Civil War between the northern Union and the southern Confederacy had begun.

JEFFERSON DAVIS

Jefferson Davis was a U.S. senator from Mississippi. He was a hero in the Mexican–American War. He also served as U.S. secretary of war before being elected president of the Confederate States of America.

1856–1859	1860	FEBRUARY 4, 1861	1861	1861	1862

APRIL 12, 1861

JEFFERSON DAVIS WAS sworn into office at Montgomery, Alabama. In his acceptance speech, Davis declared that the new Confederate States would last as a nation and would later be seen as having acted rightly.

The War Begins

The beginning of armed conflict between the Union and the Confederate states tested loyalties almost immediately. On April 17, less than a week after the beginning of the war, the state of Virginia seceded from the Union. Arkansas, North Carolina, and Tennessee would follow soon after. These southern states felt confident that Lincoln's Union Army would not win the war. The Confederate States of America now had 11 states, with a total population of 9 million.

On April 19, President Lincoln issued an order to **blockade** southern ports. The southern states relied on ships to transport goods and equipment. Now, they could not use these ports. This kept the South from having needed supplies.

UNION FORCES OUTNUMBERED Confederates about two to one in the Civil War. Today, many people learn about the Civil War by reenacting famous battles, as pictured here.

1856–1859   1860   1861   APRIL 1861   1861   1862

Division of Resources

The Confederate states were weak in many ways at the beginning of the Civil War. Their **economies** were mostly based on farming. The North, on the other hand, was very strong in the making and selling of goods.

84% of large farms in the United States were in the South.

85% of all factories were in the North.

92% of iron and steel production were in the North.

72% of railroad lines lay in the North.

29% of the U.S. population lived in the South.

The Long Fight

As the conflict escalated, Lincoln wanted to inspire the nation. He understood that the North would need many committed troops to win this war. At first, Lincoln hoped the war would end quickly, with little bloodshed. In a speech to **Congress**, he called it a struggle to maintain the government for the good of the people. His words prompted Congress to request 500,000 volunteers to join the war effort on the side of the Union.

The war did not begin well for Union forces. On July 21, 1861, they lost the Battle of Bull Run, 25 miles (40 kilometers) from Washington, D.C. After this defeat, Lincoln began to doubt that the war could be won in a short time.

During the Civil War, Confederate general Thomas Jackson earned the nickname "Stonewall." The name came from his brilliant defense against Union troops at the Battle of Bull Run. "There is Jackson, standing like a stone wall," said Confederate general Barnard E. Bee during the battle.

1856–1859   1860   1861   1861   JULY 1861   1862

BULL RUN WAS the first major battle between North and South in Virginia. The Union troops expected to capture Richmond. Instead, the Confederates pushed them back to Washington, D.C.

January–September 17, 1862

Union Offensives

By January 1862, six months of warfare had not led to an advantage by either side. President Lincoln ordered an **offensive** by the Union Army. One of Lincoln's main goals was to capture Richmond, Virginia. In early February, Union Army general Ulysses S. Grant won a series of victories in Tennessee. His forces captured two key southern posts, Fort Henry and Fort Donelson. Losing these **strongholds** was a major blow for the Confederacy.

On March 8, 1862, the first **naval** battle between steel-armored ships took place. The Confederate **ironclad** *Merrimack* battled the Union ironclad *Monitor* through the night and much of the next day. Both ships survived. Each side held the upper hand for a time, but the battle is thought to be a Union victory. This "modern" conflict changed naval warfare forever. Wooden ships were soon considered too old-fashioned and dangerous for use in battle.

During the next few months, military action increased. On September 17, 1862, a battle took place at Antietam in Maryland. There, Union general George B. McClellan fought Confederate forces led by General Robert E. Lee. McClellan was able to push Lee's forces back toward Virginia. After the battle, 26,000 men were dead, wounded, or missing. That day proved to be the bloodiest in U.S. military history.

ROBERT E. LEE

Robert E. Lee was one of the most renowned figures of the Civil War. After the war broke out, Abraham Lincoln asked Lee to lead the Union Army. Instead of accepting, Lee **resigned** from the Union Army to fight with his seceded home state, Virginia.

THE IRONCLAD *MERRIMACK* was originally a Union warship. The ship, sunk by retreating Union forces at Portsmouth, Virginia, was raised and converted into an ironclad by the Confederate Navy.

1863   1863   1864   1865   1865   1865

January 1, 1863

Spirit of Freedom

On January 1, 1863, President Lincoln issued the Emancipation Proclamation. Although the president was against the expansion of slavery, he was not an abolitionist. Lincoln viewed the war mainly as a battle over the right to secede. He used the proclamation to strike an emotional blow against the South.

The proclamation declared free all slaves in states and districts that were in rebellion. It did not affect the enslaved in loyal border states or territories that had been taken by Union forces. Despite this, the public goal of the war became gaining freedom for slaves.

The Emancipation Proclamation also led to African American troops joining the Union Army. By the end of the war, nearly 200,000 African Americans had taken part in the Union struggle against the South.

LINCOLN'S ADVISERS DID not support the Emancipation Proclamation at first. However, the victory at Antietam helped the president persuade the men to change their opinions.

| 1856–1859 | 1860 | 1861 | 1861 | 1861 | 1862 |

Freed to Fight

At the time Lincoln issued his Emancipation Proclamation, four of the nation's slave states were still part of the Union. They had not seceded with the others. These were Missouri, Maryland, Delaware, and Kentucky. Lincoln had put limits on the proclamation in part to keep these states loyal to the Union.

As northern troops continued to press toward victory, increasing numbers of slaves were freed in the South. More than 100,000 African American men from these freed regions joined the Union forces.

July 1, 1863–November 19, 1863

Battle of Gettysburg

The Battle of Gettysburg was one of the most important battles of the Civil War. It took place over three days near the small town of Gettysburg, Pennsylvania. Confederate General Robert E. Lee believed that pushing into Pennsylvania in the north, and winning a victory there, would discourage the Union from continuing the war.

Confederate troops began the attack on July 1, 1863, but the Union Army was able to retreat into a strong defensive position. The next day, Union commander Major General George Meade managed to hold the line against the Confederates. On Friday, July 3, Lee ordered Major General George Pickett and 12,000 of his men to attack the Union troops holding Gettysburg's Cemetery Hill. Known as "Pickett's Charge," the offensive failed, ending the battle.

Gettysburg was the scene of the largest battle of the Civil War. It involved 165,000 men and resulted in more than 51,000 **casualties**. The events at Gettysburg also shifted the odds firmly in favor of the North. Other important battles soon followed, with the Union gaining complete control of the Mississippi River. The Confederacy continued to weaken. Its massive loss of soldiers at Gettysburg made it difficult to fight Union forces effectively.

THE GETTYSBURG ADDRESS

On November 19, 1863, Abraham Lincoln arrived in Gettysburg. He had come to dedicate the still-unfinished Gettysburg National Cemetery. The cemetery would hold the graves of 3,500 Union soldiers who had fought on that land. That day, in just 10 sentences, Lincoln delivered one of the most moving and important speeches in U.S. history. In the "Gettysburg Address," as the speech is now known, Lincoln reminded listeners that the grave losses in battle would not be in vain because the fight was for the high cause of freedom. He also reminded his audience that the country had been founded on the idea that all people were created equal. Lincoln ended his speech by stating that "government of the people, for the people, by the people, shall not perish from the earth."

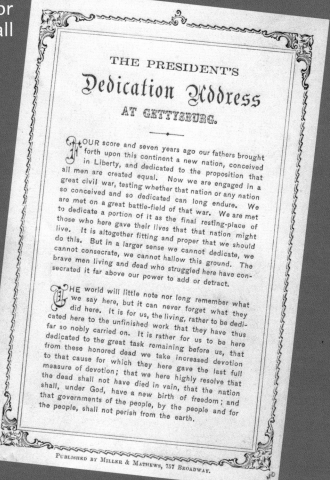

IN HIS GETTYSBURG Address, Lincoln states that "the world will little note nor long remember what we say here." In fact, as one of Lincoln's contemporaries put it, "The world noted at once what he said, and will never cease to remember it."

1863

JULY 1, 1863

1864

1865

1865

1865

NOVEMBER 19, 1863

19

Lincoln Reelected

In early 1864, General Grant began launching widespread attacks against the Confederates. By this time, he was the Union Army's commander-in-chief. On September 2, 1864, Union general William T. Sherman captured the key Confederate city of Atlanta, Georgia.

This major blow to the South helped Abraham Lincoln win a second term as president that November. He received 212 electoral votes and 55 percent of the popular vote. Sherman continued winning ground with his legendary "March to the Sea," taking Savannah, Georgia, on December 21, 1864.

WHO WAS ULYSSES S. GRANT?

Ohio-born Ulysses S. Grant won many battles for the North and played a key role in the Union victory. During the Civil War, Grant had control of a volunteer **regiment**. In a short time, he turned his volunteers into a highly trained fighting unit.

At the end of one battle, Grant earned the nickname "Unconditional Surrender" Grant. The name came from the fact that he refused to agree to any terms except "immediate and unconditional surrender."

President Lincoln appointed Grant general–in–chief of the U.S. Army on March 9, 1864. After the war, Grant was elected 18th president of the United States.

| 1856–1859 | 1860 | 1861 | 1861 | 1861 | 1862 |

IN GEORGIA, THE Confederates built a 12-mile (19-km) defensive ring around Atlanta. The 25 forts that made up the ring were crude. They did not stop General Sherman and his troops from taking Atlanta.

January 31–May 1865

End of War, End of Slavery

By 1865, the Civil War was coming to an end. On April 1, General Grant and his forces took the key Confederate city of Petersburg, Virginia. The following day, General Lee abandoned Richmond, Virginia, the Confederate capital. On April 3, 1865, Grant and the Union Army entered the city and raised the **Stars and Stripes**.

Earlier that year, on January 31, another important event had taken place. Under pressure from President Lincoln, the U.S. House of Representatives passed the Thirteenth **Amendment** to the U.S. Constitution. The purpose of the amendment was to abolish slavery throughout the United States. Three-fourths of the states needed to **ratify** the amendment in order to make it law. Almost one year would pass before this goal was achieved.

MAJOR GENERAL GEORGE B. MCCLELLAN

Nicknamed "Little Mac," McClellan was a popular leader with his troops but often at odds with President Lincoln. He led the Union's Potomac Army, but his overly cautious style cost him victories he should easily have won.

MAJOR GENERAL WILLIAM TECUMSEH SHERMAN

After his March to the Sea through Georgia, Sherman spent February through May 1865 battling victoriously through the Carolinas and on to Richmond, Virginia. Sherman was responsible for the war's largest surrender of Confederate troops.

GENERAL ROBERT E. LEE

Lee was the only man ever to serve as General-in-Chief of the Confederate States Army. The most successful of the Confederate generals, Lee avoided defeat in many battles, even with fewer men and supplies than the enemy.

LIEUTENANT GENERAL THOMAS "STONEWALL" JACKSON

Thomas Jackson was a **corps** commander of the Army of Northern Virginia. He was thought to be a heroic and successful leader. Jackson earned his nickname for his impressive defense at the First Battle of Bull Run.

MAJOR GENERAL GEORGE PICKETT

Pickett resigned from the Union Army to fight for the Confederates, joining General Lee's Army of Northern Virginia. Pickett is best known for "Pickett's Charge" at Gettysburg but was involved in many other Civil War battles as well.

Confederate Surrender

After taking the Confederate capital, Grant played a key role in forcing the surrender of Lee's Northern Virginia Army. The surrender took place on April 9, near the village of Appomattox Court House, Virginia. There, the two generals signed an agreement outlining the terms of the surrender of Lee's army. As a sign of respect, Grant allowed the Confederate officers to keep their weapons and the soldiers to keep their horses. Later that week, on April 14, Fort Sumter flew the United States flag.

The nation's mood of celebration soon turned to tragedy, however. The night the U.S. flag was raised at Fort Sumter, President Lincoln was shot while attending a theater in Washington, D.C. His attacker was actor and Confederate supporter John Wilkes Booth. Lincoln died the next morning. At the time of its greatest victory, the newly reunited nation had lost one of its greatest leaders.

1856–1859   1860   1861   1861   1861   1862

Desperate Final Days

By the end of the Civil War, scores of Confederate troops were deserting. Many wanted to get home, worried about their families and property. Farms were being emptied of crops and livestock, taken to feed Confederate troops. The Union's powerful advances were also wearing down the people of the South.

Confederate President Jefferson Davis wanted to work with Lincoln on a settlement to end the war. Lincoln refused. Lincoln told Davis that the war would not end until "it shall have ceased on the part of those who began it."

THE PLAN TO murder Lincoln also involved attempts on the lives of Vice President Andrew Johnson and Secretary of State William H. Seward. Both men survived the attacks.

A New Era

After Lincoln's death, Union forces pushed for a quick end to the war. While pockets of Confederate resistance remained, the last of the Confederate commanders surrendered on June 2, 1865. This act ended the Confederacy. In the four years of war, more than 750,000 people had died, both northerners and southerners.

By December 6, 1865, with the war over, the necessary number of states had ratified the Thirteenth Amendment to the U.S. Constitution. On December 18, the amendment became law.

The Civil War had ended. The road to abolition had been a long and difficult one, but slavery was now illegal everywhere in the United States. This was an important step forward. However, the coming years would bring further struggles, as the United States worked to uphold the ideals of freedom and equality for all.

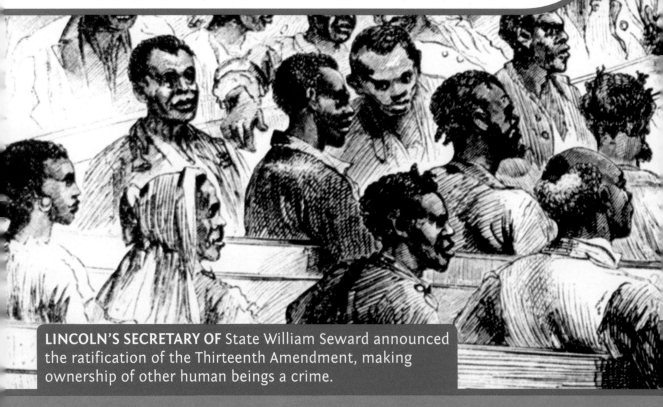

LINCOLN'S SECRETARY OF State William Seward announced the ratification of the Thirteenth Amendment, making ownership of other human beings a crime.

Activity

Create a Concept Web

Timelines are only a beginning. They provide an overview of the key events and important people that shaped history. Now, research in the library and on the internet to learn more about the Civil War.

Use a concept web to organize your ideas. Use the questions in the concept web to guide your research. When finished, use the completed web to help you write your report.

LINCOLN PUSHED for forgiveness of the South. He wanted the United States to again be solidly unified.

Concept Web

Key People
- Discuss one or two main figures who had an impact on the times, event, or person you are researching.
- What negative or positive actions by people had a lasting effect on history?

Important Events
- What significant events shaped the times or the person you are writing about?
- Were there any major events that triggered some turning point in the life or the time you are writing about?

Historic Places
- Discuss some of the most important places related to the subject of your research.
- Are there some important places that are not well-known today?
- If so, what are they and why were they important at the time or to your subject?

Causes
- How was your subject affected by important historical moments of the time?
- Was there any chain of events to cause a particular outcome in the event, time, or the life you are researching?

Write a History Report

Obstacles
- What were some of the most difficult moments or events in the life of the person or in the historical timeline of the topic you are researching?
- Were there any particular people who greatly helped in overcoming obstacles?

Outcome and Lasting Effects
- What was the outcome of this chain of events?
- Was there a lasting effect on your subject?
- What is the importance of these "stepping stones" of history? How might the outcome have changed if things had happened differently?

Into the Future
- What lasting impact did your subject have on history?
- Is that person, time, or event well-known today?
- Have people's attitudes changed about your subject with the passage of time?
- Do people think differently today about the subject than they did at the time the event happened or the person was alive?

Brain Teaser

1. What was the bloodiest battle in U.S. history?

2. What year was Abraham Lincoln first elected president?

3. What did the Confederate forces attack in the first battle of the Civil War?

4. What percentage of the American population lived in the southern states at the time of the Civil War?

5. What nickname did Confederate general Jackson earn at the battle of Bull Run?

6. What document served as President Lincoln's first major step against slavery?

7. Who was named General-in-Chief of the Confederate Army?

8. What date did Lincoln give his Gettysburg Address?

9. What amendment to the United States Constitution granted freedom to all slaves?

10. What Civil War general became the 18th president of the United States?

ANSWERS

1. Antietam
2. 1860
3. Fort Sumter
4. 29 percent
5. "Stonewall"
6. The Emancipation Proclamation
7. Robert E. Lee
8. November 19, 1863
9. Thirteenth Amendment
10. Ulysses S. Grant

Key Words

abolished: stopped or put an end to

abolitionist: people who supported the abolition of slavery

amendment: a change made to improve or add something

armory: a place where weapons are kept

blockade: to close down or prevent anyone or anything from entering

casualties: those killed, wounded, missing, or captured

civil war: a war between different groups within the same country

confederate: joined together by an agreement

Congress: the highest law-making body of the United States

corps: main division of an army in the field

economies: systems for producing and managing wealth

electoral: related to the Electoral College, a body of people representing the U.S. states who vote to choose the president

free states: Union states, before the Civil War, that did not practice slavery

friendly fire: the accidental firing of a weapon resulting in injury or death to one's ally

fugitive: a person who escaped enslavement and went into hiding

ironclad: Warships from the 1800s sided with protective armor of metal plates

naval: related to a navy or the branch of the military that conducts warfare at sea

offensive: a coordinated attack

popular vote: the votes made by regular American citizens to choose a president; as opposed to votes by the Electoral College

ratify: to formally agree to something

regiment: a military unit of ground troops

resigned: volunteered to leave a position

seceded: broke away from or left

senator: a politician who works with the state or U.S. Senate to create laws

Stars and Stripes: the United States flag

strongholds: a place that has been protected against attack

Union: referring to the United States as a country, especially in the time before and during the Civil War

Index

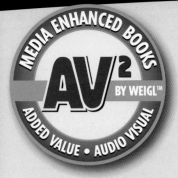

Log on to www.av2books.com

AV² by Weigl brings you media enhanced books that support active learning. Go to www.av2books.com, and enter the special code found on page 2 of this book. You will gain access to enriched and enhanced content that supplements and complements this book. Content includes video, audio, weblinks, quizzes, a slide show, and activities.

AV² Online Navigation

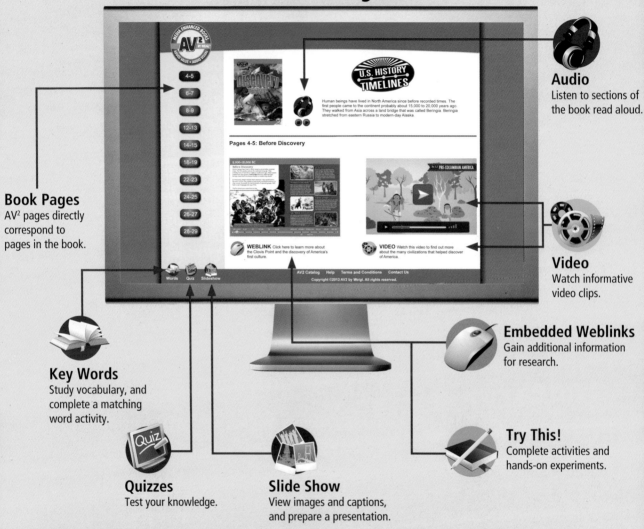

Audio
Listen to sections of the book read aloud.

Book Pages
AV² pages directly correspond to pages in the book.

Video
Watch informative video clips.

Key Words
Study vocabulary, and complete a matching word activity.

Embedded Weblinks
Gain additional information for research.

Quizzes
Test your knowledge.

Slide Show
View images and captions, and prepare a presentation.

Try This!
Complete activities and hands-on experiments.

AV² was built to bridge the gap between print and digital. We encourage you to tell us what you like and what you want to see in the future.

Sign up to be an AV² Ambassador at www.av2books.com/ambassador.

Due to the dynamic nature of the Internet, some of the URLs and activities provided as part of AV² by Weigl may have changed or ceased to exist. AV² by Weigl accepts no responsibility for any such changes. All media enhanced books are regularly monitored to update addresses and sites in a timely manner. Contact AV² by Weigl at 1-866-649-3445 or av2books@weigl.com with any questions, comments, or feedback.